For Sophie

Conversions

Oven Temperatures

Fahrenheit	Celsius	Gas Mark
275°	135°	1
300°	150°	2
325°	165°	3
350°	175°	4
375°	190°	5
400°	205°	6
425°	220°	7
450°	230°	8
475°	245°	9

US to Metric

cup	tablespoon	teaspoon	metric
1 c	16 tbsp	48 tsp	240 ml
3/4 c	12 tbsp	36 tsp	175 ml
2/3 c	10 tbsp + 2 tsp	32 tsp	160 ml
1/2 c	8 tbsp	24 tsp	120 ml
1/3 c	5 tbsp + 1 tsp	16 tsp	80 ml
1/4 c	4 tbsp	12 tsp	60 ml
1/8 c	2 tbsp	6 tsp	30 ml
1/16 c	1 tbsp	3 tsp	15 ml
--	--	1 tsp	5 ml

Text © 2020 by Danielle Kartes · Illustrations by Annie Wilkinson · Cover and internal design © 2020 by Sourcebooks
Sourcebooks and the colophon are registered trademarks of Sourcebooks. · All rights reserved.
Published by Sourcebooks eXplore, an imprint of Sourcebooks Kids · P.O. Box 4410, Naperville, Illinois 60567–4410
(630) 961-3900 · sourcebookskids.com · Source of Production: Leo Paper, Heshan City, Guangdong Province, China
Date of Production: December 2019 · Run Number: 5016834 · Printed and bound in China. · LEO 10 9 8 7 6 5 4 3 2 1

Little Chef™

Grandma and Me
in the Kitchen

This book is for

all the special times

between

_____

and

_____

Joyful recipes by Danielle Kartes
Pictures by Annie Wilkinson

sourcebooks
eXplore

Grandma, Nanna, GiGi, Mimi, Gran, Oma, Bubba, YaYa—these are all names that mean "grandmother." Whatever you call your grandma, she loves you the most. Being with each other can be such a JOY!

Cooking is a great way to spend special time together because it brings out the best in everyone. And when food is made with love, it can brighten any day. Cooking with Grandma will create love, laughter, and smiles you'll remember forever. I hope you enjoy making these fun, simple, joyful recipes with Grandma!

Follow these **SUPER** important steps to be the **VERY BEST** chef in town!

Listen well to Grandma's instructions. Cooking together is fun, but remember that Grandma cares for you and knows what's best, so listen close at every step!

Wash your hands. Clean hands make sure that no germy germs or greasy griminess make their way into your food.

Keep a clean workspace. The best chefs pick up all clutter and wipe down the countertops as they work. Ask Grandma for a clean, damp dishcloth to get started!

Never touch knives without permission. Grandma will be a big help if any food needs to be chopped!

Keep hands and arms away from hot ovens, boiling pots, and sizzling stoves. This way you won't get burned, and it gives Grandma a chance to help you by turning the heat up or down!

What's on the Menu?

In this book, you'll find simple, delicious recipes for you and Grandma to make together. Each recipe includes ways to personalize it. Do you and Grandma love raspberries more than blueberries? No problem! Make raspberry muffins instead. This is your special time together. Use what you love or use what you have on hand!

Breakfast
Best-Ever Buttermilk Blueberry Muffins

Apple Cinnamon Overnight Oats

Beverage
Strawberry and Orange Slushy

Lunch
Easy Peasy Tomato Soup and Toasted Triple Cheese Sammies

Warm and Toasty Ham and Cheese Rolls

Dinner
Inside-Out Creamy Stuffed Shells with Turkey and Broccoli

Chicken Tortellini Soup

Side
Grannie's Special Creamed Corn

Snack
Fruity Fruity Strawberry Fruit Dip

Cinnamon Sugar Popcorn

Dessert
Very Berry Short Crust Cobbler

Banana Cake with Cream Cheese Frosting

Extras
Tips on how to make memories together

Conversation starters and jokes

Celebrate the every day

Write in your own favorite recipe

Making Joyful Memories Together

Cooking along with Grandma will help you both to create new and wonderful traditions! Here are some ways you can make your time in the kitchen special.

♥ Do you like to listen to music? Pick a fun song you and Grandma enjoy that can be played each time you cook together.

♥ Try wearing matching aprons, chef's hats, or shirts!

♥ Work together to decide who gets to collect what, who gets to crack the eggs, and who gets to taste test as you cook!

♥ Use a special mixing bowl or spoon that can only be used when you're working in the kitchen together.

♥ Eat your food on fancy dishes (if you want to)!

Want to hear a funny joke?

What does a nut say when it sneezes?

"Cashew!"

How do you make a milkshake?

Put a cow on a roller coaster.

Why do fish swim in salt water?

Because pepper water would make them sneeze!

Why couldn't the butter leave the casino?

Because it was on a roll!

What's a scarecrow's favorite fruit?

Strawberries.

Hee-hee!

Ha-ha!

Apple Cinnamon Overnight Oats

Makes 4 servings   **V**   Prep time: 10 minutes + 8 hours chilling time

Sleepover at Grandma's? Right before bed, mix up a batch of these tasty no-cooking-required oats and enjoy a delicious breakfast in the morning!

Equipment

Large bowl or container
   with lid
Wooden spoon

Ingredients

1 cup rolled oats
1 apple, peeled, cored, and
   finely chopped
2 tablespoons brown
   sugar
¾ cup whole milk
¼ cup cream
½ teaspoon cinnamon
Pinch of salt

1 This is a magic recipe! All you need to do is mix everything up in a bowl or container with a tight-fitting lid and leave it in the refrigerator overnight! In the morning, you will have delicious apple cinnamon oatmeal to enjoy with Grandma!

For a chocolate version, add 1 tablespoon cocoa powder and skip the apples!

Use any fruit you love!

Serve warm with a pat of butter by microwaving your portion 30 to 45 seconds.

Strawberry and Orange Slushy

Makes 4 servings (V) Prep time: 5 minutes

This is THE BEST! Slushy, slushy time! Pull up a chair and have Grandma grab the blender and lid.

Equipment
Blender

Ingredients
2 cups ripe strawberries, tops removed

1 cup ice

2 cups orange juice

1 tablespoon lemon juice

1 to 2 tablespoons honey

1 Everything on the list goes into the blender! Put the lid on and ask Grandma to help you turn the blender on. It's gonna get loud! Blend the ingredients up until nice and frosty smooth. Next, pour into cups and enjoy! Easy, right?!

Frozen fruit works great too!

Use any fruit juice you have.

No honey? No problem. Just skip it!

Easy Peasy Tomato Soup and Toasted Triple Cheese Sammies

Makes 2 quarts of soup and 4 sandwiches **V** Prep time: 10 minutes **V** Cook time: 20 minutes

Equipment

Stock pot

Large mixing bowl

Stick blender or traditional blender

Frying pan

Spatula

Plate

Ladle (if using a traditional blender)

Ingredients

For the Soup

4 tablespoons butter

1 medium yellow onion, roughly chopped

1 (28-ounce) can whole peeled tomatoes
   in juice

3 fresh tomatoes, chopped

4 cups low-sodium chicken stock or broth

3 cloves garlic, smashed

½ cup sweet basil, chopped

Salt and pepper to taste

½ cup heavy cream

For the Sammies

8 ounces cream cheese, softened

2 cups cheddar cheese, shredded

1 cup mozzarella, shredded

Salt and pepper to taste

½ teaspoon onion powder

8 slices of bread

Butter for the pan

1. Set your stock pot on the stove. Add the butter and ask Grandma to turn the heat to medium. Once the butter is melted, add the onion. Cook until the onions are translucent—that means a little see-through! Add the rest of the soup ingredients except the cream, and simmer for 20 minutes.

2. While the soup simmers, put the cheeses, salt, pepper, and onion powder into a bowl and mash it up with a fork. Ask Grandma to heat the frying pan up to medium heat.

3. Spread a little butter on the outsides of two bread slices, then spread your cheese mixture gently on the inside. Repeat this process until you have four sammies! You are a toasted cheese sammie machine!

4. With Grandma's help, put one sammie in the pan. Cook one side until it's crispy and the cheese is melting, then flip and do the same on the other side! Remove from the pan and set aside on a plate.

5. Ask Grandma to remove the soup from the heat. Blend 2 to 3 minutes with the stick blender in the pot, or ask Grandma to carefully ladle the soup into a blender. Once it's smooth and ready for dunking, pour the soup back into the pot. Add heavy cream and stir it up. Serve your soup with the toasted triple cheese sammies, and you are in for a delish lunch!

No blender? No problem! Swap out the can of whole tomatoes for crushed tomatoes, and serve up a chunky tomato soup.

Skip the grilled cheese and add cooked tortellini to the soup.

Gluten free? This will work great with your very favorite gluten-free bread!

Add any cheese you have to the cheese mixture!

Want the soup dairy free? Use olive oil instead of butter and skip the heavy cream.

Add any cooked ground meat to the soup and skip the blender for a hearty stew.

Warm and Toasty Ham and Cheese Rolls

Makes 4 servings ⓥ Prep time: 10 minutes

Equipment
Baking sheet
Parchment paper
Small bowl
Spoon or rubber spatula

Ingredients
4 bread rolls, sliced in half
1 tablespoon mustard
¼ cup mayonnaise
12 ounces sliced deli ham
4 slices cheddar cheese

Use any bread, cheese, or meat you like!

Top your sammies with crunchy pickles, lettuce, or tomato!

1. Preheat the oven to 375°F with Grandma's help. Cover the baking sheet with a sheet of parchment paper.

2. In the small bowl, mix the mustard and mayo together and spread just a bit on the inside of every roll. Divide the ham and cheese among the four rolls.

3. Place the sandwiches on the baking sheet, and ask Grandma to put them in the oven. Bake 10 to 15 minutes until the cheese is nice and melty and that roll is oh-so-toasty! Ask Grandma to take the rolls out of the oven, and serve alongside crunchy chips and sliced veggies such as carrot sticks and peapods!

Joyful Moments

When we're together sharing a meal or just having a snack, it's a great time to connect. Here are some questions for you to take turns asking each other to get your conversation going!

♥ What is something that made you smile today?

♥ If you could go anywhere in the world with me, where would you pick?

♥ How were you kind to someone today?

♥ What's your favorite memory with Grandma so far?

♥ What's your favorite thing about yourself?

♥ What would you do if you found the pot of gold at the end of a rainbow?

♥ What is your favorite food?

♥ What was your favorite meal to eat when you were little?

Chicken Tortellini Soup

Makes 4 servings ⓥ Prep time: 10 minutes ⓥ Cook time: 15 to 20 minutes

Equipment
Stock pot
A big appetite!

Ingredients
2 (32-ounce) cartons
　(8 cups) chicken stock
2 celery ribs, chopped
2 carrots, chopped
1 small yellow onion, chopped
1 chicken breast, sliced as
　thinly as possible
½ teaspoon black pepper
Kosher salt to taste
1 16-ounce package fresh,
　prepared cheese tortellini
　pasta

1 Add the chicken stock, veggies, and chicken breast to the soup pot. Ask Grandma to turn the heat to medium and bring everything to a simmer. Cook about 10 to 15 minutes.

2 Once the chicken is cooked through and veggies are tender, season with pepper and salt and carefully add the tortellini. Careful not to splash—the soup is hot! Cook 3 to 5 minutes. They cook extra fast because they are fresh. Serve with bread and butter and a nice big salad. Yes, chef!

Use any fresh stuffed pasta such as ravioli or fresh unstuffed pasta, if you wish!

Skip the meat for a noodle-y delight!

Use vegetable broth, if you prefer!

Add lots more veggies or anything else you love!

Grannie's Special Creamed Corn

Makes 4 servings ⒱ Prep time: 15 minutes ⒱ Cook time: 15 minutes

Equipment

Large bowl
Tiny bowl
Large skillet
Wooden spoon

Ingredients

5 ears of corn
1 tablespoon butter
Salt and pepper to taste
1 cup heavy cream
½ cup Parmesan, shredded

1 Place the small bowl upside down inside the big bowl. Looks silly, but wait till you see this trick! Have Grandma stand a corn cob on its end atop the upside-down bowl and slice the corn off the cob. The big bowl catches all those kernels! Repeat with each ear of corn.

2 Melt the butter in the skillet over medium heat. Let Grandma help because it's hot!

3 Add the corn to the skillet and gently stir. This is the perfect time to season with salt and pepper!

4 Add the cream and Parmesan cheese, then cook until it's thick and bubbly. My little chef friend, you just made fresh, delicious creamed corn.

Use any veggies you love. This recipe works wonderfully with spinach, peas, and even zucchini!

Fruity Fruity Strawberry Fruit Dip

Makes roughly 2½ cups ♥ Prep time: 10 minutes

Some combinations are almost too good to be true: cream cheese and honey, fruit and this dip, and Grandma and you! Now you can have all three at once. Make this dip and be thankful for all the perfect combos in your life.

Equipment
Hand mixer
Mixing bowl
Spoon or rubber spatula (optional)
Serving bowl (optional)

Ingredients
8 ounces cream cheese,
   softened
1 cup heavy cream
½ cup strawberries, chopped
2 tablespoons honey,
   or more if you'd like it sweeter

You can pick just one fruit or all the fun fruits to dip! Here are some fruits that love to be dunked:

- Apples
- Bananas
- Strawberries
- Orange slices
- Grapes
- Pears

1 Grab a hand mixer, the best mixer of all (well, besides you and Grandma—you two might be the best mixers of ALL time)! Add the cream cheese, cream, strawberries, and honey to a large mixing bowl. Start your mixer on low speed. If it's a little heavy, ask Grandma to help you steady the bowl and mixer. As the mixture mixes, it will start to get fluffy. The heavy cream is turning to whipped cream! Mix this until its light and fully whipped and you can't see any chunks of cream cheese. It should be nice and smooth!

2 Use a spoon or rubber spatula to move the dip into a serving bowl, or you can just leave it in the bigger bowl—no problem!

3 The final step is to use your clean pointer finger for a taste test! Remember, no double dipping! Does it need anything? Now is the time to add more honey or fruit or cream.

No strawberries? No problem! Use any juicy berry you have: blackberries, blueberries, or even raspberries work great!

Don't want to dunk anymore? Chop up the fruit you have, and mix it together with the dip! This makes the yummiest fruit salad! You can bring some home to Mommy or Daddy.

Want a chocolate dip? Add ¼ cup hazelnut spread and 1 tablespoon unsweetened cocoa powder to the original recipe. Delicious!

No heavy cream? Well, fruit-flavored yogurt works wonderfully! Simply put an 8-ounce container of your favorite yogurt in with the cream cheese. It won't be as fluffy, but it's every bit as yummy.

Cinnamon Sugar Popcorn

Makes 4 cups **V** Prep time: 6 minutes

Equipment
Large bowl
Small bowl

Ingredients
1 bag plain microwave
    popcorn
1 tablespoon butter, melted
¼ teaspoon cinnamon
1 tablespoon granulated sugar

1 Ask Grandma to follow the microwave popcorn instructions while you stir the cinnamon and sugar together.

2 Once the popcorn is popped, pour it into a nice big bowl (careful, it's hot!) and drizzle that melted butter all over the top! Then sprinkle on the cinnamon sugar.

3 Sit somewhere and ask Grandma her favorite stories about when she was little. Or make a list of each of your favorite movies and watch them together! Popcorn makes everyone happy!

CELEBRATE!

Every day can be special. It doesn't have to be a holiday or your birthday; **YOU** are special and that is a reason to celebrate! When we wake up each morning feeling grateful for the day, it gets very easy to have a heart for celebration.

Here are some ways you can celebrate:

♥ Bake a cake! Any day is a good day for cake!

♥ Go for a walk and spot all the different flowers and trees! Bring back a bouquet of the prettiest flowers. Or gather fallen leaves or interesting rocks!

♥ Ask Grandma what her very favorite meal was when she was your age! Maybe you can make that meal together!

♥ Make a card and draw pictures in it for somebody you love!

♥ Sometimes, just asking your family if there's anything you can do to help around the house can make their day!

You are the perfect person to find the joy in the every day. At breakfast, lunchtime, snack time, dinnertime, or even dessert, talk about all the **joyful** moments together at the table.

Banana Cake with Cream Cheese Frosting

Makes about 12 servings **Y** Prep time: 15 minutes **Y** Bake time: 25 to 35 minutes

Move over, banana bread—banana CAKE is here! It's light and fluffy with the yummiest frosting, perfect for celebrating every day you're with Grandma!

Equipment

2 large mixing bowls
Wooden spoon
9-x-13 cake pan
Hand mixer

Ingredients

For the Cake

2 to 3 tablespoons butter, chilled
4 ripe bananas (with brown spots, please! Brown spots mean a banana is extra sweet!)
⅓ cup vanilla or plain yogurt
1 cup dark brown sugar
½ cup granulated sugar
½ cup butter, melted
2 eggs
2 tablespoons oil
2 teaspoons vanilla extract
1¾ cups flour
1 teaspoon baking powder
½ teaspoon baking soda
½ teaspoon kosher salt
½ teaspoon cinnamon

For the Frosting

8 ounces cream cheese, softened
3 cups powdered sugar
½ cup butter, softened
½ teaspoon vanilla extract
Pinch of salt

1 Butter your 9-x-13 baking dish with the chilled butter. You can use your fingers to squish the butter into the corners! Just remember to wash your hands after you're done.

2 Ask Grandma to preheat the oven to 350°F. Peel the bananas, dump them into the mixing bowl, and smash 'em up real good with a fork. Next, add the yogurt, sugars, melted butter, eggs, oil, and vanilla into your bowl and mix like the wind!

3 Next, dump in that flour, baking powder, baking soda, salt, and cinnamon. Mix everything up until just combined— no overmixing!

4 Pour the batter (with Grandma's help) into your baking dish and bake 25 to 35 minutes until it's golden brown and cooked all the way through. Ask Grandma to take the cake out of the oven to cool while you make the frosting.

5 Add the frosting ingredients to a clean mixing bowl. Gently, on low speed, mix all the ingredients until smooth. Careful now, powdered sugar loves to fly around the kitchen if you go too fast! Once your cake is completely cool, frost it up!

Skip the frosting if you'd like!

For chocolate banana cake, in place of the 1¾ cups of flour, substitute 1½ cups flour and ⅓ cup unsweetened cocoa powder.

Add ½ cup chopped walnuts for extra crunch.

It's your turn! Make up your own recipe together or write down the recipe for one of Grandma's specialties.

Our ♥ Recipe

Date:_____

_____

Serves:_____ Prep Time:_____ Cook Time:_____

Equipment

_____
_____
_____
_____

Ingredients

_____
_____
_____
_____
_____
_____
_____
_____

Directions

_____
_____
_____
_____
_____
_____
_____
_____
_____
_____
_____
_____
_____
_____

Why we love it: _____ ♥